PIANO/VOCAL/GUITAR

BILLY JOEL

52ND STREET

Additional editing and transcription by David Rosenthal

ISBN 978-1-5400-1455-9

HAL•LEONARD®

Visit Hal Leonard Online at
www.halleonard.com

Contact us:
Hal Leonard
7777 West Bluemound Road
Milwaukee, WI 53213
Email: info@halleonard.com

In Europe, contact:
Hal Leonard Europe Limited
42 Wigmore Street
Marylebone, London, W1U 2RN
Email: info@halleonardeurope.com

In Australia, contact:
Hal Leonard Australia Pty. Ltd.
4 Lentara Court
Cheltenham, Victoria, 3192 Australia
Email: info@halleonard.com.au

FOREWORD

52nd Street was Billy's first album to top the Billboard charts. Released in 1978, it was the second album produced by Phil Ramone and it yielded three Top 40 hits ("My Life," "Big Shot," and "Honesty"), two Grammy Awards (Album of the Year and Best Pop Vocal Performance – Male), and a Grammy Nomination for Song of the Year ("Honesty"). It would later become the first album ever to be released commercially on CD.

Coming off the breakthrough success of his 1977 album *The Stranger*, Billy was feeling very confident. He had gone from playing clubs, theaters, and colleges to headlining arenas. Creatively though, he was determined not to replicate *The Stranger*. He decided to try something different by hiring jazz musicians to enhance the band and bring their influence onto the record. It worked perfectly, inspiring Billy to push the boundaries of his songwriting and bring his music to a new place. Some examples are the sophisticated chord structures of "Rosalinda's Eyes" and the jazz sections of "Zanzibar" featuring solos by legendary trumpeter Freddie Hubbard.

Having played keyboards in Billy Joel's band since 1993, I have an inside perspective into his music. Accordingly, Billy asked that I review every note of the sheet music in his entire catalog of songs. As a pianist, he entrusted me with the task of correcting and re-transcribing each piece to ensure that the printed music represents each song exactly as it was written and recorded. This is the latest edition in our series of revised songbooks in the Billy Joel catalog, which began with *The Stranger* songbook back in 2008.

The challenge with each folio in Billy's catalog is to find musical ways to combine his piano parts and vocal melodies into playable piano arrangements. First, the signature piano parts were transcribed and notated exactly as Billy played them. The vocal melodies were then transcribed and incorporated into the piano part in a way that preserves the original character of each song.

Although each verse of "My Life" sounds similar, there are subtleties in the piano accompaniment and in the arrangement that change from verse to verse. All of the verses have been written out, rather than using repeats, in order to capture the subtle differences in the vocal melody and in the piano answers. On the original recording it fades out, so I added an optional ending, which is how we play it live.

Billy's Fender Rhodes part on "Rosalinda's Eyes" plays a big role in the character of the song. There are subtle changes in his voicings on each of the verses, so here again I wrote out each verse in its entirety to preserve these differences. On the record the flute and marimba parts vary slightly each time the main riff returns, and this is reflected in the written piano parts in the sheet music.

The characteristic horn lines on "Half a Mile Away" have been included through most of the song. In some places the horns overlap the vocals, but both are written out wherever possible so that the essence of the character of the song is preserved. The unison horn soli section is accurately transcribed and made into a playable piano part.

"Until the Night" was recorded in the style of the Righteous Brothers as a tribute to their music, which Billy loves so much. For the choruses I wrote piano voicings that capture the vocal harmonies and preserve the integral character of those harmonies. The climactic sax solo after the bridge has been captured into a playable piano part.

The classic intro and ending piano parts in "Honesty" are written exactly as Billy played them, and "Stiletto" has all of Billy's signature piano solos transcribed note for note. The ending of "Stiletto" fades out on the record, so I added an optional ending, which is how we play it live.

All of the songs in this collection received the same astute attention to detail. The result is sheet music that is both accurate and enjoyable to play, and that remains true to the original performances.

Billy and I are pleased to present the revised and now accurate sheet music to the classic album *52nd Street*.

Enjoy,

David Rosenthal
January 2019

BIG SHOT

Words and Music by
BILLY JOEL

Fast Rock 'n' Roll

Well, ___ you went up - town rid - ing in your
all im - pressed ___ with your

lim - ou - sine, ___ with your fine Park Av - e - nue clothes. ___ You had the
Hal - ston dress, ___ and the peo - ple that you knew at E - laines, ___ and the

You had to have the {front page, bold type,} {white hot spot - light} you had to be a big shot last night. Whoa. Oh, oh, Whoa. Oh, oh, Whoa. Oh, oh, oh, Whoa. Oh, oh, oh Whoa.

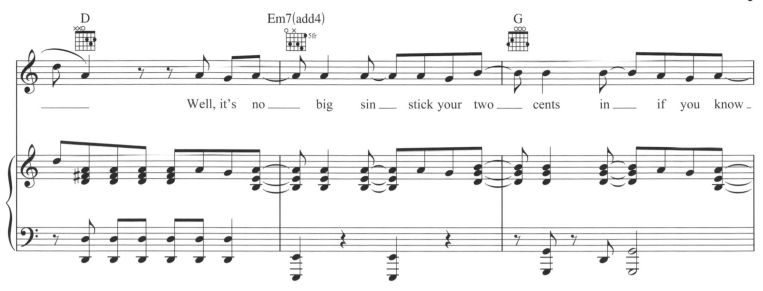

Well, it's no ___ big sin ___ stick your two ___ cents in ___ if you know ___

___ when to leave it a - lone. ___ But you went o - ver the line, ___ you could-n't

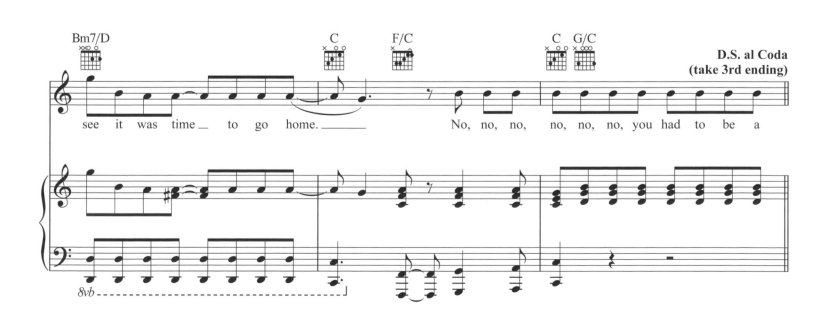

D.S. al Coda
(take 3rd ending)

see it was time ___ to go home. ___ No, no, no, no, no, no, you had to be a

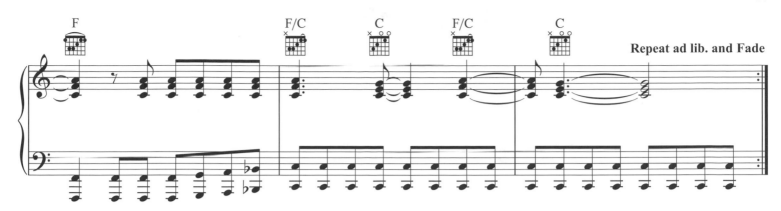

Repeat ad lib. and Fade

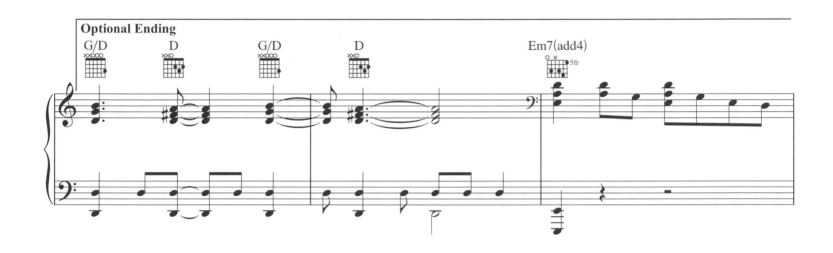

Optional Ending

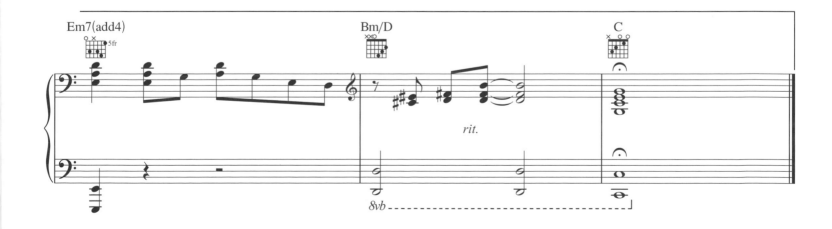

HONESTY

Words and Music by
BILLY JOEL

If you ___ search for ten-der-ness, ___ it is-n't hard to find. ___
I can al-ways find some-one to say they sym-pa-thize ___

You can have the love ___ you need to live. _____
if I wear my heart out on my sleeve. ___

But if you look for truth-ful-ness you might just as well ___ be blind; ___ it
But I don't want some pret-ty face to tell me pret-ty lies _____

MY LIFE

Words and Music by
BILLY JOEL

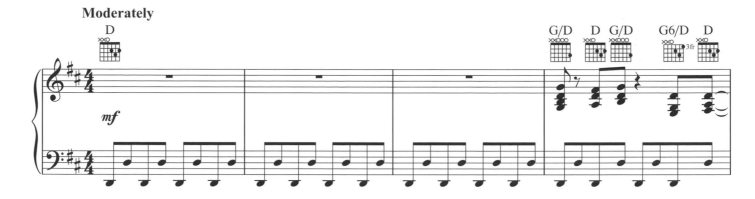

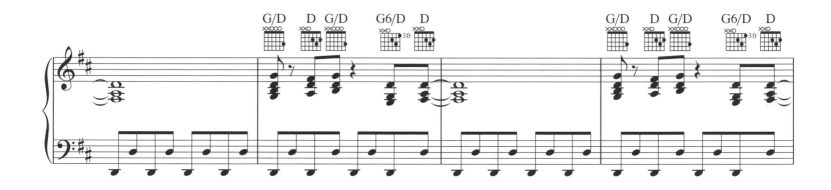

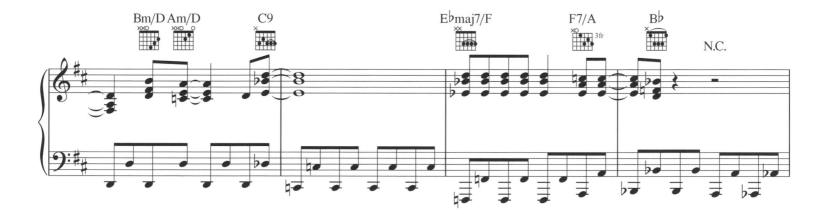

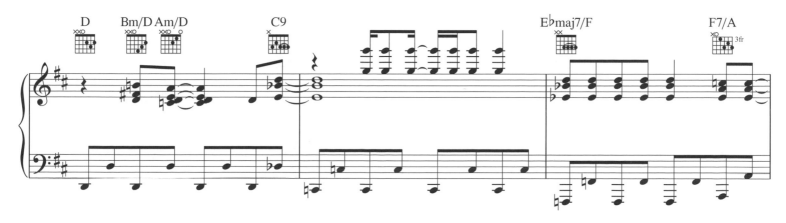

Now he gives them a stand - up rou - tine in L. A.

I don't need you to wor - ry for me 'cause I'm all

not on my time. *Piano Solo*

I don't care ___ what you say ___

___ an - y - more, ___ this is my life.

Go a - head with your own life, leave me a - lone.

(Lead vocal 1st time only)

Keep it to your-self, it's my life.

Repeat and Fade

Keep it to your-self, it's my

life.

Optional Ending

Keep it to your-self, it's my life.

ZANZIBAR

Words and Music by
BILLY JOEL

CODA

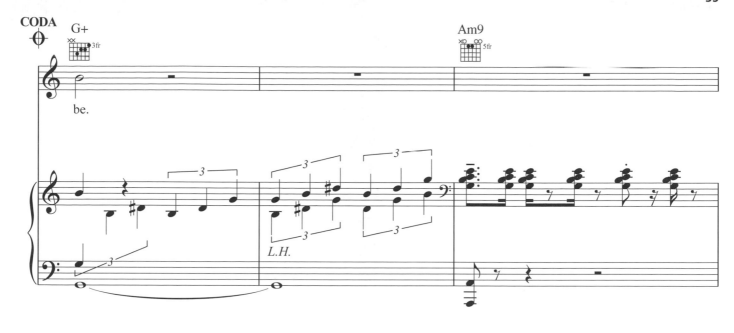

Double time Swing feel

Optional Jazz Solo

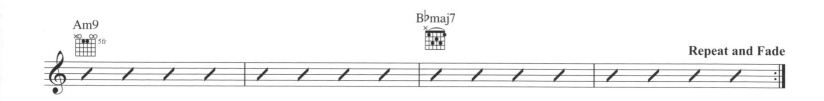

Repeat and Fade

Optional Ending

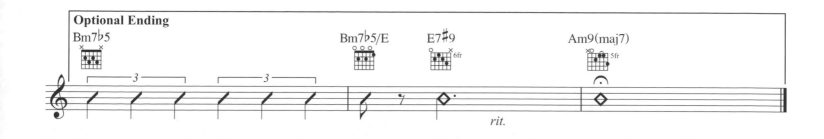

rit.

Big Shot

Well you went uptown riding in your
limousine with your fine Park Avenue clothes
You had the Dom Perignon in your hand
And the spoon in your nose
And when you wake up in the morning
with your mouth on fire and you're
eyes to bloody to see
Go on and cry in your coffee
But don't come bitchin' to me

chorus I {
Because you had to be a big shot
Didn't you? you had to open up your mouth
You had to be a big shot didn't you?
All your friends were so knocked out
you had to have to last word last night
you know what everything's about
}

And now you just don't remember
All the things you said
And you're not sure you want to know
I'll give you one hint honey
You sure did put on a show —

You had to be a big shot didn't you?
You had to prove it to the crowd
You had to be a big shot didn't you?
All your friends were so knocked out
You had to have the last word last night
You're so much fun to be around
You had to have the front page, bold type
You had to be a big shot last night

Inst.

Honesty

If you search for tenderness
It isn't hard to find
You can have the love you need to live
But if you look for truthfulness
You might just as well be blind
It always seems to be so hard to give

chorus: Honesty is such a lonely word
Everyone is so untrue
Honesty is hardly ever heard
And mostly what I need from you

I can always find someone
To sympathize
If I wear my heart

Rosalinda's Eyes

I play nights in the Spanish
Part of town
I've got music in my hands
The work is hard to find
But that don't get me down
Rosalinda understands

Crazy latin dancing solo
Dawn in Herald Square
Oh Havana I've been
Searching for you everywhere
And though I'll never be there
I know what I would see there
I can always find your Cuban skies
In Rosalinda's eyes

When she smiles she gives
her love to me

Half A Mile Away

Little Geo is a friend of mine
We get some money and we buy
a cheap wine
Sit on the corner and have a holiday
Hide the bottle when the cop goes by
Talk about women and lie, lie, lie ...
My other world is just a half a mile away

Wait for mama to turn out the light
Crawl on the roof and then I
hit the night
I should be sleeping but tonight
I just can't stay
I've given everybody so much time
But now I need a moment that's mine
My other world is just a half a mile away

4 X mmm — It's just a half a mile away

Angelina save a place for me
I've been livin someone else's life
And now I've gotta be free

Until The Night

I never ask you where you go
After I leave you in the morning
We go our different ways
To seperate situations
It's not that easy anymore

Today I do what must be done
I give my time to total strangers
But now it feels as though
The day goes on forever
More than it ever did before

chorus:
Until The Night, Until The Night
Oh I just might make it
Until The Night until The Night
When I see you again

Now you're afraid that we have changed
And I'm afraid we're getting older
So many broken hearts
So many lonely faces
So many lovers come + gone

STILETTO

Words and Music by
BILLY JOEL

She
She

When she says she wants forgiveness (it's) such a clever masquerade.
Then she says she wants affection while she searches for the vein.

She's so good with her stiletto,
She's so good with her stiletto,

you don't even see the blade.
you don't really mind the pain.

You don't see the blade.
You don't mind the pain.

To Coda

She cuts you hard, she cuts you deep. She's

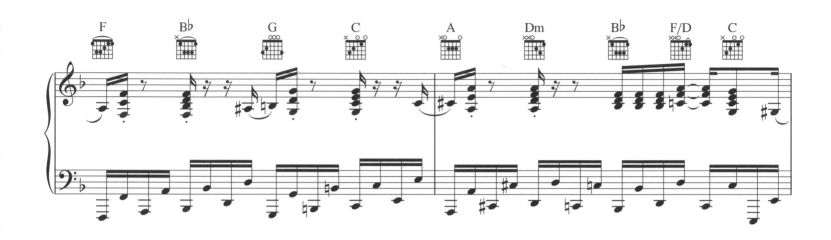

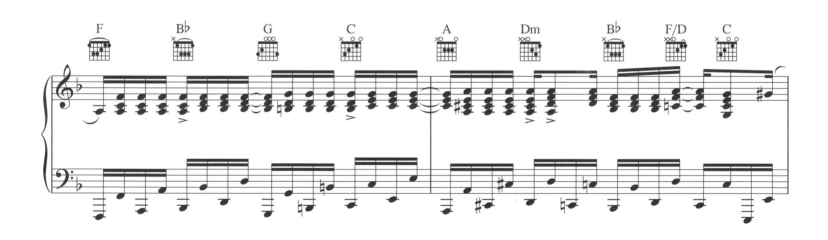

ROSALINDA'S EYES

Words and Music by
BILLY JOEL

HALF A MILE AWAY

Words and Music by
BILLY JOEL

Lit - tle Ge - o is a friend of mine. We'll get some mon - ey and we'll

UNTIL THE NIGHT

Words and Music by
BILLY JOEL

-ing.
-gers.
-er.
-an.

We go our
But now it
So man-y
To - day we'll

dif-f'rent ways ___ to sep-'rate sit - u - a - tions. ___
feels as though ___ the day goes on for-ev-er,
bro-ken hearts, ___ so man-y lone-ly fac-es,
be un-sure; ___ is this what we be-lieve ___ in?

1, 3

It's not that eas-y ___ an-y-more
so man-y lov-ers ___ come and gone.

52ND STREET

Words and Music by
BILLY JOEL

Slow Funk, with Swing 8ths, in 2

They say it takes a lot to keep a love a-live.

In ev-'ry heart there pumps_ a dif-f'rent beat.

But if we shift the rhy-thm in-to

o-ver-drive,_____ well, we could

gen-er-ate a lot of heat. On Fif-ty-